C000186766

Panya Banjoko is a UK-based writ
internationally, coordinates a write
patron for Nottingham UNESCO (
Her work has featured in numerous anthologies including
the award-winning *Dawn of the Unread* series published by
LeftLion magazine in 2016. In 2017 her poem 'One of a Kind'
was commended in the Writing East Midlands Aurora poetry
competition and her poem 'They and Them' was featured in
an exhibition by artist, academic and critic Keith Piper at the
Beaconsfield Gallery, London.
She received the Women in the Arts Poetry Award for
Outstanding Achievement in 2008 and the Black Achievers
Culture, Music and Arts Award for her work as a poet in 2017.

Some Things

Panya Banjoko

Burning Eye

BurningEyeBooks
Never Knowingly
Mainstream

This edition published by Burning Eye Books 2018

www.burningeye.co.uk

@burningeyebooks

Burning Eye Books
15 West Hill, Portishead, BS20 6LG

ISBN 978-1-911570-42-4

Printed & bound by ImprintDigital.com, UK

Some
Things

CONTENTS

The Others 9
Some Things 10
Hummingbird I 11
One of a Kind 12
When Art Speaks 14
Riot 15
Dirty Gold 16
They and Them 17
Quicksilver 19
Birds of a Feather 20
Living Without Proof 21
When Mother Sees 23
Airport 24
Brutes 27
I Know Something 28
Hummingbird II 29
Reverie 31
Family Ties 32
The Night Before 33
Fresh Meat 34
Bowled Over 35
Walk the End 36
Wondering 37
The Maker 38
Vow 39
Time Factor 40

Tradition   41
Mother's Reason   43
Capitalists' Dream   46
If We Are Lucky   47
Hummingbird III   48
Stones   50
Windowless Doors   52
All Sorts   53
The Art of Love   54
Making Our Way   55
Better Things   56

THE OTHERS

They judge your guts
even before you've had a chance
to spill 'em.

SOME THINGS

Some things are meant to be lost,
like a shifting state in loopholes
consumed by thunderstorms
clacking under the weight of rain.

Some things cannot be collected,
like a tank of confusion
or a shelf of hatred
or a landscape of gravelled love.

Some things are boxed up,
like tensions between bodies
that stand in spotlit rooms
near pebbled paths that cultures cross.

And some things are hard, as memories
or splinters made from rocks
that demarcate borders
until nature reveals its secret (or not).

HUMMINGBIRD I

When Toad met Snake they chuckled.
Neither feared the other, neither cared for the other.
They played, side by side; venom bound their friendship.

When they saw Hummingbird looking at half moon,
they planned to topple him, made a pact as tight as a gourd
to bind loose vines into a snare.

They invited Hummingbird to a party
full of jam-tart-sweet nectar and coral bells,
told him how fine his ruby-red throat shone in the sun.

Come sing, said Snake, who could turn words inside out.
Come eat, spat Toad, soaking his victim like rain.

When Hummingbird was sipping butterfly bush juice,
Snake said his wings needed preening, Toad agreed.
Hummingbird had never been told this before.

They fetched their tools, sharpened them whilst he sang,
told Hummingbird to spread wings so they could see his beauty,
promised to leave them splendid and smooth,

then sliced them clean   dragged them to the edge of the forest,
buried them under mouldy stench,
left Hummingbird to wither like leaves in putrid pool.

Without wings, Hummingbird was mute,
his beauty gone, his song like a prayer gone.

Snake and Toad chuckled…

ONE OF A KIND

They had kept him, seven long years
hidden behind a crumpled wall
in a cavernous shelter, set like a cage.

When the King ordered, they fed him
mildewed bread, made him drink the milk
of rancid yaks, waited for his skin to turn pale,
for his voice to leave him.

Then, when he was eager for water
to dislodge the sand in his throat,
they promised him life for his stint,
set him to work.

They told him, *Use your fingers*
like the limbs of a Darwin's bark spider,
make beauty like purple lilies
and the call of the shuffle-wing bird.

With tools laid out like surgeon's instruments
he performed his vision.
Pounding like the call of a woodpecker,
he softened and formed thick ingots of gold
into sunbird tails.

Hands bent, nails jagged, he gripped tweezer
between finger and thumb,
planted gems in rows like marching ants;
with each new tide he cut, pierced and soldered.

When he had shaped his dreams into curves,
when he could see the image of his face
in the gleam of the dome,

when he knew it could not be matched,
he inscribed it with timeworn text and it was done.
The King called his people

to behold the work of the master craftsman
and they revelled with delight at the skill in his bones,

then they cut off his hand.

WHEN ART SPEAKS

With brush I paint the snatch squad in blue,
squash militant berries to make the red,
flecks of gold to cover the scars.

Against a backdrop of magenta
I stain sloping views
with the drunken face of bulldogs.

With dye, thick like sludge, I dab
until the canvas turns to mire
to hide the binding of your body
in fifty feet of tape
in front of infant son,
gagged until you choke
on the vomit they baptise you with
as they bite you on the cheek,
send you back in a van.

RIOT

They
said
that Tuesday
as striding silhouettes
saluted the air
that the hole
in his
padded jacket
caused torches
to flame
travel the country
and the feathers
as they
spurted
glided
kite-like
and
skittered
in the
August blue
twirling
as they fell
into a
mass
burial
ground.
All of us
stared
at our screens
watched
as truth
lay quarantined
waiting
to become
an Oscar-wining
remake.

DIRTY GOLD

At fourteen he chips away at the orb
to escape, he plays seek and find
for £3 a day, descends makeshift mine
twelve metres deep, through dusty shaft
an arm's length wide. Each sweat-soaked hour
he dreams of sparkling water.

He tiptoes up crumbling wall,
surveys his find,
powders and filters it with mercury,
watches barehanded, as dust combines
into splendid silver balls.

A faceless goldsmith, he works
so sister sleeps without cradling hunger.
Labours as open pits gulp the earth,
teak drawers hide in lavender bellies
last year's gleaming rings and shiny neckpieces.

THEY AND THEM

They had big houses in the City,
unlike Them,
who lived in ramshackle patches on estates.

They ate saffron fish with jewelled rice.
It was normal for Them
to go hungry.

When Them
started saying
They were cousins,
seeds of the earth,
They should share,
They hurled punches,
smashed bottles on heads,
beat Them
raw.

Sometimes when They battered Them
it made Them
feel like putting an exit bag over their heads.

They made Them
build prisons and museums,
poached objects,
made Them
with clamped mouths fill the galleries.

One day, it was too much for Them.
With oiled throats,
voices the colour of mandarin fish
could be heard across the broken roads.

When the sounds became shapes
They ordered Them
to be quiet.
When the shapes became the butts of bayonets

17

They ordered Them
to stop.

When the butts became handles
They became frantic,
feared bayonets with cutting edge.

So They made up stories,
wicked stories,
about Them
stealing children and eating their toes.

When that wasn't enough
They said that the tails at the back of Them
would strangle women,
but the women liked the tails of Them.

They grew angry,
shoved all of Them
into prison and released the wolves,
cut out the wombs of the women,
salted the insides, fed Them
to the pack.

That was the last They heard of Them.

They were content, picking their teeth.
They didn't see
out of the ruins of a doorless haunt,
crawling, cockroach-like
on two bent, bloody legs,
was one of Them.

QUICKSILVER

After the shine
crept
down
his face,

prayed for a moment

in his throat,

sat on his shoulder,

crouched

before it seethed,
settling in his chest

between the spokes of his ribs,

tore the pit of his gut,
punched holes
into his groin,
his thighs,
his ankles,
his soles,
spilling
onto the cracked asphalt,

she'd heard it was a hard stop.

BIRDS OF A FEATHER

In the murk of the city, where stone lions guard,
Blackbird builds nest from plants mixed with mud,
lined with grass, and preens his coal-black feathers.

Magpie roosts in tall tree, surveys windmill on the breeze,
chirps, *This is a city we're all proud of*, tail held high.
On the horizon, he swoops in between branches,
parting songbirds from their melodies.

Blackbird keeps distance from Magpie, all seasons.
Magpie descends in nines and tens, skimming hedges,
ripping flesh from bone, leaving bloody shells.

With flutelike song, Blackbird begs for his unhatched brood,
says, *We feel pain the way you do*, hops, flies,
perches on branch, waits for answer.

In cluttered concrete jungle, before the cacophony of dusk,
after the rain has fallen, they meet. A gang of black and white
boasting metallic-blue sheens, they sit in council and deliberate.

On the third day Magpie offers reprieve. Blackbird
cannot believe his chance, no more senseless slaughter.
As one, then two, three days pass he leaves nest to find fat
worm.

Razor-beaked Magpie dives and strikes, dagger claws shred
feather and flesh, laughs at babies shrieking,
defenceless hen screeching in plaintive high-pitched grief.

With open bill and inclined head, wings and tail spread,
Blackbird picks up dead body of baby, drops it at Magpie's feet,
says, *You promised a truce.*

Magpie with beady eye surveys castle on the hill,
shiny trinkets in its belly, sings, *My onyx friend,*
I never promised I would not tell a lie.

LIVING WITHOUT PROOF

or worry
or simmering rage
or noose around necks
or you're actually pretty!
or where are you from?
or no, where are you from?
or no, *really*, where are you from?
or I adore reggae
or you must have a big one
or I love fried chicken
or whaddup girlfriend!
or you've got rhythm
or you're so urban
or is that your hair?
or ain't even gonna ask but gonna touch it?
or how did you get here?
or I'd love to visit Africa!
or you're good at sport
or a chip on your shoulder
or being three times as good as
or six times more likely
or threat in numbers
or stalked in shops
or first like me you've met
or alone in the village
or the object of gaze
or the odd one out
or I don't see colour
or excrement posted
or whitened CVs
or the state of things
or no green lights
or crushed air
or imperial weight
or first-class measures
or fractured justice
or cardboard spoons
or covered in scars

or fitting the description
or stop and search
or no Acts will change this
or keep your nose out
or keep your kind out
or go back to your own
or asphyxiated truth
or plot and destroy
or where's the weed
or curated disharmony
or mothers weeping
or hard stops
or morning murders
or tainted days
or bruised cheeks
or bruised communities
or angry women
or you're not like most…
or not like them
or I'm not racist
or my best friend's one
or you're really so nice
or no room at the inn
or you're so articulate
or how should I sound?
or you don't look ghetto
or far too aggressive
or over-the-top anger
or happy-go-lucky
or how do you know?
or you're killing us
or you're killing us
or no really you're killing us
or never being able to change a damn bloody thing.

WHEN MOTHER SEES

She shakes both legs,
her calves and ankles
and toes bending
upwards,
until she has enough leverage
to set her spine
and crawl in a frenzied strobe
with tears
near someone's knocked door.

It takes more than minutes
to breathe reason
over phone line jerks
with shipwrecked legs.
Eventually
silence falls
at 3.45am
and the smell of blood sets.

AIRPORT

The muted tones of people
anxious to get their movements done
hum like a tired choir.

Black screen above my head
flashes boarding gate 29 for flight EZY2433.

Leopard-print travel bag, coat and iPad
deposited between two grey trays.

Today's the day they'll see beyond the surface.
See I wear my granddaughter's smile
to keep me upright,
my daughter's hope to keep me breathing.

Hijab-clad elderly woman sets the buzzer squealing.
If Reuters have done their work
I should pass without a blink.

Today's the day I'll pass through
if they don't see me
like I see them seeing me.
I know I'll have taken a stride
if they don't see me
like they were raised to see me.

Each time she enters the machine
it betrays her anxiety,
squeals like a banshee.

Handheld detector scans hijab
for hidden bombs and detonators.

Today's the day I'll pass through
'cause I'm tagged out in jeans from Bench
and a sweater from Gap that blends in,

shows some assimilation has taken place.
I speak without much of a Jamo twang.

Security clerk feeds trays through scanner
like clockwork toy.
He fires French in my direction
without looking
although I know he sees me flinch.
Je ne comprends pas, I reply
before his translation knocks me flat.
Take off my hat?

I spy hijab woman fumbling to put on shoes.
They've handled her plenty.

If I were Kate Middleton
before she met Prince William,
would this happen to me?

I can only speculate,
do probabilities, percentages, ratios, guess.

He orders me to stand to one side.
His gesture says, *You have yet to see the extent of man
and his doings.*

He makes me stand like Christ,
arms outstretched. Children stare at my shame.

He pats my right leg
from thigh to ankle,
my left, from ankle to thigh,
each arm, from the pit to the wrist,
rubbed down.

He runs his thumbs around the waist of my jeans,
under the rims of my breasts,

down my spine,
then he squeezes the eighty-two dreads
curled to an eighth of their size
in my knitted black hat.

He squeezes in between the coils,
squeezes like he's milking a cow,
nothing but Samson's strength rests here.

After two phases of what floats by
I'm taken behind the scene
to meet her, The Supervisor.
She puts people in their boxes,
asks who I am.

I'm an artist, I write words,
turn them into poems and songs,
paint stories with parables and proverbs,
sing speeches.
I have nothing more to declare.

She orders me to remove my coat,
my jeans,
my faded underwear
so she can see,
explains she doesn't wish to invade my privacy
so she asks me to do her work
and I oblige
because of the citizen I was raised to be.

I use my fingers
to spread my behind wide
for her to see.
And as the architect of power signals my dismissal
I leave behind the shame
but take with me the words.

BRUTES

They do not fear the steel of a woman.
Sat near bushes, armed with spears,
they beg her to come.

I KNOW SOMETHING

The best thing I have ever done,
as I forward to the next stop,
where the doors are not open
to the realms at the bottom,
is to keep going, not falling.

When I am not with luck
the most I can do is roll the dice
as Adam sings
it has always been this way.

I will become only what they are
in temples reaching the moon
yet travelling behind in the mood
of right circumstances.

While the wheels skid
I am me.

HUMMINGBIRD II

Before Hummingbird shrouded himself in undergrowth,
before he asked why Snake and Toad had dismembered his
wings,
before he accepted he would be food
for sharp-shinned hawk
soon,
very soon…
even before his courage sunk like filthy swamp
and drifted
down,
Ant red as berry crawled onto Hummingbird's back,
measured the wound, and said the Oracle had sent her,
sent her to find him under weeping tree,
sent her to bathe bloodied stumps in dew-soaked leaves,
sent her to make wings new.
Hummingbird listened but could not speak.

Between the shadows
Ant called friends to find reeds and plants and gum.

Day after day they plaited,
poked stems through holes,
used tree bark and root and sap,
entreated orb web spider to bring diaphanous thread
with a playful soul
and he spun fan-shaped wings
with sticky strands beaded not smooth.

They covered the bark and the roots and the twigs
after Spider twisted fine cords of fibre into thoughtful grace.

When they had made wings, long and elegant as nectar jewel,
they fitted them at midnight
beside the river that ran through towns,
fixed them tight,
held Hummingbird still.
When moon had slept twice,

they formed a circle.
Ant said, *It is time.*

Hummingbird spread wings and fluttered,
voice staccato at first,
he hovered and stuttered,
voice shrill,
he soared and muttered,
higher he flew until the rattle became
a splendid baritone,
then vanished with a zip.
Ant called after him,
What will you do now you are new again?

Hummingbird chuckled…

REVERIE

Last night I was feeding dreams
in a place over summer
where tribal statues prayed.

I was making stew for small dogs
with horns, that barked,
nipped at the ankles of women.

When I asked what I should do,
a seagull with talons on its arms
constructed a room for me.

In this room, standing on all sides
was my father, with the head of an owl,
cable tied to keep it straight.

With a large beak, he said, *The race is short.*
Why not leave it, to reduce its weight?
It would make sense to shuffle off the board.

FAMILY TIES

Me and my family look good on photos.
Even the police wouldn't get mad at us.

We get away from places, put red dots on the map,
make sure we fill up with ought-to. We crawl

through holes in upper right corners and out of a box
if the chase gets like falling headfirst into a wall.

Me and my family like closed curtains, cubbyholes,
backyards where we can bury eyes.

THE NIGHT BEFORE

That night, I dreamt
the earth's surface cracked.
Lava destroyed me.
I ventured into the city, sat on a roof,
encountered thuggish types.

I thought, they'll kill me.
Turns out they wanted to finger me instead.
His friend was first
to show me how he liked it.

I went back to the house,
washed thumbs from my tongue,
spit from my neck.
Went to bed, lava eroding
the base of my skull.

That morning, downstairs,
I fell onto Mum's lap.
She was right.
I wasn't behaving like war
but like collapsed lungs.

She was holding my head
when she asked what was wrong
and I said I'd had a nightmare.

FRESH MEAT

His father visited again last night
smelling of old soles and menace.

He tears young flesh apart, spears it
onto skewers before searing.

He didn't scream when he was seasoned
in the damp cellar.

When he doubles in size, he will become
a chef like him. Just. Like. Him.

BOWLED OVER

He stands me up,
then shouts,
except this shout
says

CUNT.

The whole crowd of his fingers
curl into bowling balls
as he flicks his wrist,
propels fist,
then strikes
until he clears me out.

He knocks me
down,
sets me up, wobbling,
aims, ready
to knock me down again.

WALK THE END

I get out into the chaos
more hours than a day,
turning corners, hanging
off balconies, riding the guards.

I slink through streets,
heart suspended on crutches,
pride waving
from the back of buses.

When I'm done at ground level
I use the middle of my hand
to slap my forehead,
make sure I'm real.

WONDERING

Morning's dream
was on a bus
slacking
through a maze,
waiting
for a prince
to sit beside me,
tell me he's sorry
he missed our night.
I would say OK,
I was fine,
then ask
if he knew
where to get off the bus
in this maze.

THE MAKER

When he wove, words became cloaks
maidens sought.

Pin-neat hands beat the weft
with the dyed weight of his past.

When the warp was cloaked in red
waiting to be hemmed, hung

with hawk-eye care, he crammed the wall
with hearts he took.

VOW

When dawn pricked the edge
of his sloped-down terror
he surrendered himself to the prey
that stuffed Saturday-night quarrels
into his mouth.

When all things became some things
he gathered himself, full of whine,
and walked down the aisle.

TIME FACTOR

4 he tried to cut her open
6 he finally did

13 she denied knowing
16 regret kept her awake

19 it didn't matter
21 it did

25 the dreams endured
29 she tried to forget

30 she tried to forget
33 she tried to make peace

36 she would hate forever
48 she
51 still
66 hates.

TRADITION

The birth
beside her father
mapped the start.

The wraith of a mother
crawled and screamed,
bared her teeth.

The grandmother
silenced the mother
by plugging her throat.

The people that saw
folded their arms,
sang umms and ahhs.

Prayed for the blood,
the stump of a name,
the bones of a jaw,
the snarl of an eye,
the step of a life,
stuff skulls are made of.

The grandmother
crossed her heart,
scratched her feet,
buried the tender afterbirth.

In my dreams, she said,
I eat until my teeth fall out.
Blink until I am sick.
Sit up in bed,
burrow until I am ahead.
Bludgeon sleep,
watch as mothers weep.

The baby
cursed the stork
before it slept,
used fingertip to poke
between the snores,
stretched hands
with the vigour of life,
pinched the night awake.

The grandmother said,
Shirk as you saunter,
speak as you stretch,
tie your hands,
pull them closer to pray,
speak at night to moonlight
and if sorrow survives
in front of you
then say
Amen.

MOTHER'S REASON

When the swell put its arm around her,
turned her into an overweight wrestler,
kept her captive, until it was time to juice her,
squeeze her dry,
it turned her life inside
down.
When she sank
below
she said she was sad, not fed up.

At 2.30am
when pupils were pinpricks,
babies craved coddled eggs,
she saw fifteen baby cows.
Their wellingtons squelched in the mud.
She shouted for them to pull her out
but they tried to stop her,
so she lay down with doubt.

When she sat talking to the window,
toppled over by the past,
she called for Hope,
but only three horses came:
Barry,
Snowdrop,
Bumper.

People don't change; they just get bigger!
said Bumper.

When he gave up his superhero job for her
she said,

TOO BAD I HATE BEING AROUND PEOPLE WORTH NOTHING
JUST AS MUCH AS I HATE THREE-TIERED SHOES,
SEQUINS ON TROUSERS
AND TRUTH THAT SMELLS LIKE OLD LADIES' FALSE TEETH.

She stuck her tongue out at the highs
as they said goodbye.

When dirty dishes and crumpled clothes lay like broken bones,
forks without teeth,
knives without edges
sliced the cares on her cheeks,
she prayed for Hope,
but it scurried down a pit.
She dangled possibilities and yesterday's dreams to entice it
but it wouldn't come out.

When she fell asleep at 3am,
woke at 3.05
smelling pan-fried tomatoes and plantain spears
on one of those gurgle-along low days
that gobbled her up where she sat,
she couldn't imagine a life of pristine surprises,
just couldn't.

When none of the superheroes that visited
had powers
(always left before dawn)
weekends were work,
workdays were torture,
so she split herself into six
to share some of her with all of them.

Some ate.
Some kicked.
Some punched.

When she put herself back together again
there was one piece m i s s i n g.

When one day started
before the other had ended

– the gurgle became a moan

- the superheroes were all gone

- the brandy turned to rage

- the crumpled clothes became mountains

- her cheeks were all shredded

- the nights never came

- the days always stayed

- the doctors had lost Hope

- there was nothing more to say.

CAPITALISTS' DREAM

I eat the world
and never get sick of it.

IF WE ARE LUCKY

Three feet and a furlong deep,
my aunt believed if it ticked
then the tock would follow.

Three wooden kegs she had
depending on the time
being filled with not anymore.

She carried a musket
under her nose when she bled
and the heads she counted
around the table she sat at
were not all the same.

The last was useless,
the first was a waste,
the one in the middle
left without grace.

They were all bundled up,
packed with rum
and layers of sauce.

When she was asked
would she do it again
she said of her vice, *Somethings
should never be done thrice.*

HUMMINGBIRD III

He hummed
bold yellow hums
with lilac frills.

He swept
through the air,
thanked Spider for help,
Oracle for vision,
Ant for her care.

After,
much later after,
back to dry bark home after,
to sloping branch shelter after,
tender twig feet gripped again,
upside-down and back again,
round and round and round again,
until the swell of home
under his wings
beamed bright as a new day.

Home.
Sweet sapsucker well.
Home.

Hummingbird stopped.
Motionless
there   in midair.
In marshes
broad and bent
sat Snake and Toad
with dragonfly's wings on their breath.

Hummingbird remembered
the days he stuttered,
nights he bled,
with voice small said,
Remember me?

Even air stood still
as Snake and Toad gazed
at the majesty of Hummingbird's wings.

They slurped,
Come sing.
We missed your melodies.

LIAR!

shouted Hummingbird.

LIAR! he said.

Tail beat air until it was singed,
rage blotted out the sun,
he bellowed,
One life I'll spare.
The other is mine.

CHOOSE!

He watched
as each pushed the other forward,

watched
as each blamed the other,

watched
as they poked, plotted and choked,

watched
Toad bite Snake,

Snake gash Toad,
spitting and hacking
until eyes slapped shut
and the days of time were done.

Hummingbird flapped his wings
and chuckled…

49

STONES

can be hammers
smacking placards
into tainted lawns
can sing
to a hail
of we shall overcome
be a fairytale
father's dream
of children
trekking
through woods
on scattered paths
to the slap
of a stepmother's snarl
like sugar skulls
can be decorated
painted
into homes
line boot trays
used by hoary crows
to raise limits
arm small hands
fix them for war
the brave
load slingshots
defeat giants
who give orders
to sledgehammered chain gangs
as they pulse
under searing heat
constructing
palaces
paths
circles
and walls
break bones
over

and
over
and
over
again
from talisman
to burial item
make-up
to medicine
one to kill two birds
seven to hide bleating kids
hear them rumble
tumble
aged and rolling
like the wise
philosopher
they charm
with the weight
of those who churn
and scrum
with phoney plans
they break moods
when you take stock
they leave a taste
bitter
that sticks in your throat
like a stone.

WINDOWLESS DOORS

When the great white whale appeared, I thought
there may have been gods, but it never spoke.

When I took a step back, my foot slipped
off the dirt track, caused me to stumble.

When I tumbled through the forest
I landed in front of a house without walls.

When I buried my eyes under a bridge
the windows floated near shallow streams.

When I swam towards the red boulders
the doors gloated around my side.

When I looked at me and didn't sing
I barked like a must-fight boy.

When the boulders were behind
I hid where trees were deep with green.

When I looked back and rolled uphill
I saluted the ground covered in leaves.

When I saw bones smothered in prints, I knew
the house I buried belonged to the hound in me.

ALL SORTS

A few try to shelve things in the crooks of doors
or stick them in the back of green-covered journals.

Others try to coax the stay with signs marked open,
even as doors close.

Over a grey phone line, some crank open mid-afternoon,
prime it with glum, run on toes through the past.

Some fall before speaking, some speak at length,
some drink to remember, some drink to forget,
some wait for lows to turn high.

Some, from fear of being within, trap the shame;
make friends with misery, hold their breath,
begin to think normal is possessiveness.

Even slack jaws don't set them apart as they say
it's better than nothing.

There are a few, after a while, that do get round to leaving.

THE ART OF LOVE

You
had me
the moment
you mixed the oils,
then coaxed the canvas
tight on your wooden frame,
reloaded your brush to blend
the rusty fragments of peeled paint,
buttery strokes smoothing tilted lines.
When I dry… you paint me over again.

When you collect and archive the remains,
survey the smudges your fingers make
on layers of head-strong fibres,
weak-kneed under the weight,
preserving the moment,
currents of colour
declare their stay,
sit in frame
binding
me.

MAKING OUR WAY

The key was in.
He controlled the speed,
racing full throttle.

Heading towards the station,
he crashed.
I was still a mile away.

We strolled to the subway,
then he went down, to my place,
where I needed his head to be.

BETTER THINGS

She waited,
rehearsed her prayers
with holy water,
sequinned puff voice,
polite as a nun's habit.

She told him
she was more than a Black girl
with a gang of children,
more debt than teeth.

He was the fourth
this season,
a drunken slurp
stuck like tar to ground.

Each day…

She prayed.
He slept.
She prayed.
He roamed.

One evening
she gave him kola nut.
He did not chew it.

She prayed.
He slept.
She prayed.
He roamed.

She told him,
Don't talk back.
He did.

She prayed.
He slept.

She prayed.
He roamed.

She told him
he could not stay.
He laughed.

She was too tired
to spin colours.

The next day
too tired
to trek to market.

The next day
too tired to work.

After he ate yam porridge
seasoned with thyme
she stared at the walls.

She waited.
Her pulse quickened.

She waited more.
Her tongue wagged less.

She waited
for the wait to stop,

then used stone, like drum,
to beat him.

She waited.

For the next to come.

THE OFFERING

Fifty-four days later
she swept away the debris,
slumped at the place marked X,
bent down on both knees,
kissed the ground with her forehead.

Had it been fifty-three days
it would have been too soon.
She had returned, six times,
to look for it, the egg-like structure
that shone like the Procyon star.

After the first crossing they moaned
it was too hard to capture.
With shoulders hung low
against the thrashing rain
she walked the seas, commanded
the waves to fold, knew the axis
just needed a nudge.

Fifty-four days later, she released it
on the imposing blue, a mist
of molecules that suffocated terror,
gave the world back its glimmer.
They had a lot to learn
from this thing called faith.

VISION

Trekking across the country,
stopping at a castle,
wrestling three nights,
waking the fourth morning,
putting his quarrels into a bag,
securing it tight,
asking the people
wearing masks with beaks
how best to breathe,
was a peasant.

He nodded
when the people pointed,
walked through the wooden gate
on the pebbled path
down a scowling slope
under branches of slouching trees
until he reached a clearing.

There, a sparrowhawk,
its head poised for hunt,
smoked bark
scented with lemon,
stood with 200 feathers in its tail
in colours from grey to blue,
and on its warped back
were pools of eyes
that moved like synchronised dancers,
eyeing him up and round.

Tell me, said the peasant
how do I breathe here
where the air is tight
for it threatens to crush my nose?

It opened the hatch
concealed in its wing,

pulled out a scroll and read,
For thousands of years people have asked
how to temper air.
Always it lay beside them,
always in their grasp.

It flung the scroll back into the hatch.
The eyes they smiled and blinked.

The peasant asked again,
How do I breathe here?
For it screams in my ear,
prickles my gum,
paints a limp in my gait.

The sparrowhawk squawked,
flapped its wings and said,
I share with you this.
Breathe quick,
you'll be hunted by the gulls;
breathe shallow,
they'll bury you in sand
right up to your neck.

Behind its head, one eye opened
for the peasant to see
a meadow tall and green
and growing in abundance.
Flowers of every shade
stood off in the distance;
trees filled with apples
that waited to be picked.
The light from the sun's stretch
cast shadows the colour of honey
that swayed this way and that.

The peasant fell to the ground,
lay there, looked up at the sky,
said, *This is the place I have dreamt of*
when bellowing like a whale.

The sparrowhawk lifted one scaly foot
from which ten rats emerged.
They grabbed the bag,
gobbled it down with a gulp.

It closed its eye and said,
Let the rays warm you within,
every leaf and fold of your heart,
to the stem of your soul.
Now, breathe deep, my friend,
breathe deep like a ravine.

Acknowledgements

Thanks to Ashira for being a great source of inspiration, Abs for the critical listening and marvellous meddling, Asha and Amani for ensuring I stayed focused. Many thanks to Sharon Monteith for taking the time to proofread and to Keith Piper for front cover design and the laughs in between.